T0016854

What Others Are Saying...

THE TOPIC OF ABORTION is so charged. It is incredibly valuable to hear from someone who has experienced it. Thank you, Denise, for your courage and transparency. I well remember how difficult it was for you to first articulate the events. What an encouragement to walk with Denise through her story and be reminded of how God heals and forgives and the beauty that comes from sharing our brokenness, causing others to know that they are not alone, and they are not without hope.

—Stephanie Cordis

MEETING DENISE THROUGH A divine connection was no coincidence! Reading her story was no coincidence, either! Her story captured my heart right away, making it difficult to put down. Her story is hard, but with God's power, His love, and His healing, Denise has received her voice back. Her heart's desire is to use her story to tell others that they too have a voice. I recommend this book because you will be inspired and captivated by a heart that knows heartache but has come through it victoriously.

—Jacque Murphy
Executive Director
Deeper Still, Freeing the abortion wounded heart

Restored for HIS Glory

Denise Venturini-South

Restored for HIS Glory

FROM DISGRACE TO GRACE,
A PATHWAY TO FREEDOM & FORGIVENESS

Denise Venturini-South

SAVAGE PRESS

Restored for His Glory

Published by Savage Press
506 Second Ave. Suite 1400
Seattle, WA 98104 www.johnsavagegroup.com/savage-press

ISBN: 978-1-958211-28-1 (PB)
ISBN: 978-1-958211-21-2 (HB)
ISBN: 978-1-958211-22-9 (ebook)
Library of Congress Control Number: 1-11906106711

Cover design by Amber Weigand-Buckley – barefacedcreativemedia.com
Interior design by Faithe Thomas – MasterDesign.org

Printed in the United States of America.
10 9 8 7 6 5 4 3 2 1

Contents

Foreword....................ix
Introduction....................xi
Chapter 1 — A Guiding Light....................1
Chapter 2 — Longing for Relationship....................9
Chapter 3 — Childhood Trauma....................13
Chapter 4 — New Beginnings....................21
Chapter 5 — Pain and Lasting Grief....................29
Chapter 6 — Out on the Ledge....................35
Chapter 7 — Motivated to Help....................41
Chapter 8 — Sweet Perfume....................51
Chapter 9 — Saving Grace....................61
Chapter 10 — Making All Things New....................69
Chapter 11 — Elizabeth's Story....................77
Chapter 12 — Healing and Provision....................83
Chapter 13 — The Watchman....................91
Chapter 14 — God's Truth Revealed....................95
Chapter 15 — How to Press On....................103
Chapter 16 — Set Free....................107
Appendix A....................111
What's Next....................115

Dedication

This book is dedicated to my children:
Gazelle, Jason, Nismah, Anna, Elizabeth,
and those who have no name.

Acknowledgments

Christopher South
Author and award-winning journalist,
friend, and a brother in Christ.

Stephanie Cordis
My sister in Christ, friend, and confidante.

Foreword

THE FRIENDSHIP WAS QUITE unexpected....

My daughter asked if one of her lifeguard friends, Anna, could stay at our house for ten days so her mother would only have to make one trip north to drop off her two daughters at different colleges. I hesitated slightly but decided to do it.

Anna's mom, Denise, needed to stay one night at the house, too, before she headed back home. It turned out that we had an enjoyable time, and afterward we invited Denise to stay with us whenever she came to pick up her daughter.

Although formerly strangers, we shared a love for the Lord and our daughters were friends at the same college. As early risers, we found ourselves sharing and laughing over a cup of coffee and breakfast. At the time, I was still processing a recently-revealed family secret. As she listened to me, she slowly revealed that she had a secret, as well ... and she felt the Lord wanted her to be open about her secret. Denise told me it was extremely important to her that her children hear the secret from her first. God was creating in Denise a burning desire to use the pain and knowledge from her secret experience to minister to others. But what of the pain it would cause her children?

Such a dilemma.

Each time Denise came to the house we would talk about it and pray about it. How could God want her to hurt her children? What if they rejected her because of the secret? It was months before Denise even trusted me with the actual secret—one layer at a time. It had been so embedded and carefully guarded that it took time to be put in words. But it must be put into words—to be spoken and written for others to hear and read—to reach hurting people with the healing power of a loving Savior.

— Stephanie Cordis

Introduction

Two things stand out from a recent newscast on changes in abortion laws in Chile. One pro-choice supporter described the process of aborting an unborn child as "disturbing the pregnancy." In the same article, a woman who was forced by her family to have an abortion talked about its long-term effects.

"Abortion scars you for life," she said. "In my case, if I had the choice, I would have had my daughter. But it wasn't my choice. Abortion scars you for life—before and after. Nothing good comes out of abortion—nothing, nothing."[1]

Obviously, this woman considered her abortion to be much more than simply disturbing or interrupting the pregnancy. For her, it was a very traumatic experience. How many of the women who represent the 58 million abortions conducted in the United States since the Roe v. Wade decision in 1973 have had feelings like hers? Or how many feel nothing because our society teaches that having a choice is more important than life? I often wonder how

---

1 BBC News, September 29, 2016 by Reeta Chakrabarti article – "Chile's president defiant over abortion changes."

many women who are pro-choice supporters have had an abortion.

I have my own story to tell on this subject, and it was not easy to tell. However, the need to tell my story began when I felt God convicting me of the necessity of sharing my story with others—mainly with women and men who have gone through the experience of an abortion (because men share in the experience) or who are contemplating abortion.

As a Christian, I was quite familiar with the story of Abraham, who had been told by God that he would be the father of a great nation. Abraham and his wife Sarah were childless for many years until the birth of his son Isaac. Yet, when Isaac was a young teen, God told Abraham to sacrifice his son on an altar. I thought about that Bible story when I considered writing this book. To me, it would be like putting my own children on an altar—an altar of hurt. I didn't want my children to share the hurt caused by my own experience in aborting my unborn children—something I did three times after feeling the negative pressure of family members or my spouse. I believed the guilt and anguish I felt, even years later, would undoubtedly cause my children great pain. They might never forgive me! How could God expect this of me, and could God heal them and take away their pain?

As someone suffering with post-abortive stress syndrome (PASS), those thoughts and many more raced through my mind constantly. At the same time, God was making it apparent to me that the next step in freeing me from the guilt and shame I felt was to write this book. If I intended to share my experiences with others in this way, then it was necessary for me to first share this story with my children.

I decided I had to accept God's promises as revealed in the Bible as true—that God is faithful despite my shortcomings and dark past. I believe God's promise that He will take every bad situation and turn it into good for His purposes, as He told us, "And we know that all things work together for good to those who love God, to those who are the called according to His purpose" (Rom. 8:28 NKJV).

That was it. If God said He would take my guilt and pain born out of my ugly past and use it for good, then I would be willing to expose what I consider to be a very personal and shameful part of my life in order for others to understand the lifelong trauma that results from killing your unborn child.

The commission was to give comfort to others as God has comforted me.

> **Blessed be the God and Father of our Lord Jesus Christ, the Father of mercies and God of all**

> **comfort, who comforts us in all our affliction, so that we may be able to comfort those who are in any affliction, with the comfort with which we ourselves are comforted by God. For as we share abundantly in Christ's sufferings, so through Christ we share abundantly in comfort too.**
>
> —2 Corinthians 1:3–5

This affliction can refer to both outward circumstances and inward state of mind—a mind deceived into thinking abortion is best and then living with the secret of shame and disgrace.

My hope and prayer for this book is to turn your attention to the One who is able to heal you, use you, and make you whole. May you find indefinable and inexpressible joy which only comes from knowing God as you grow in the knowledge of Him, our wonderful Father, and Savior Jesus Christ.

> **Those who sow in tears shall reap in joy. He who continually goes forth weeping, bearing seed for sowing, shall doubtless come again with rejoicing, bringing his sheaves with him.**
>
> —Psalm 126:5–6 NKJV

• CHAPTER 1 •

A Guiding Light

THERE WAS A YOUNG girl, a virgin, who was tricked by her brother into entering his bedroom to bring him food. However, when she brought it to him, he refused to eat. Instead, he violated her even though she begged him not to. He would not listen to her and proceeded with the abuse. Once he was done, he hated her. Her life was destroyed by the abuse heaped on her by her own brother. She ended up as a desolate woman living in her other brother's house and is never heard about again. This sounds like something that happens today, but this story is from 2 Samuel 13 in the Bible. Abuse is not new to our generation.

To be desolate is to be ruined, bleak, and depressingly empty. I can relate to Tamar's story and am sure there are others who can relate as well. That was her story; this is mine.

The emptiness that results from abuse caused me to seek love and acceptance all my life. What I didn't realize is that the kind of love and acceptance I was seeking could only come from God through a relationship with His Son, Jesus. It took years and many poor choices for me to discover this truth.

Life was scary and dark at times during my childhood. I wish I could say it was idyllic, but it was not. Born in 1960, I was too young to be part of the 60s turbulence. The Staten Island, New York, neighborhood where I lived was typical of the era. My home was a three-story colonial; the bedrooms were on the third floor and my bedroom was sandwiched between my parents' and my older brother's, who was six years older than me. I vividly remember the rag rug on our porch where I spent a lot of time alone playing with my dolls, often making them clothes out of old dishrags.

My happiest moments were spent in church. When I was five years old, I thought nothing bad could ever happen there.

One Sunday morning when I was five years old, my mother and I went to church together, as was our custom. Standing on her right side, I said, "I always want to feel this good," while glancing up to see her face.

Without even looking at me, Mom said, "That's impossible."

It is possible, I told myself, trying to block any thoughts that would disturb the peace I felt. Maybe it was a child's naiveté, a kid's reasoning, but I loved going to church. I loved how I felt going to church. I even loved the day, Sunday, because it was a special day.

Compared to Saturday, typically a day for chores and television, Sunday was a holiday. My father worked a second job painting houses on the weekends, so he was rarely home, and my mother sometimes spent Saturdays alone in her bedroom with the door closed. On Sunday mornings, though, I woke up anticipating attending church, a place I knew I would feel good. And that started with looking good.

I loved how I felt going to church. I even loved the day, Sunday, because it was a special day.

Part of my family's church ritual included laying out our church clothes on Saturday night. And our family—well, my mother and me, since my brother and father didn't attend church with us—dressed up to go to church. It was important in my family to look extra special on our First Communion and when we were confirmed. After

Confirmation, we were regular members, and my mother and I always dressed up.

My dad was a Korean War veteran, and though he never went to church, he said he knew God better than anyone. I guess he was referring to what he saw in the war, but he never elaborated. I asked him once if he believed in God during the war, and he commented that everyone had faith during the war. Fighting was fierce and tragic; fear abounded; many prayers were said in foxholes and many tears were shed—and heard.

My father did say that the Roman Catholic Church had changed, and indeed it had. In the mid-to-late 60s, Mass began to be said in English rather than Latin. Some Catholics never got over that. I don't know what my father felt about it. He just said that he believed in God in his own way.

My mother took me to church on Sundays because she felt it was her duty. Each Sunday morning, my mother and I took the ten-to-fifteen-minute walk from our home to our local church. She believed my First Communion and Confirmation would get me to heaven.

Going to Mass was a cultural norm for my family. Italian Catholics went to church, and that's what my mother and I did.

Following my eighth-grade confirmation, I began walking alone to church on Sundays. As a child I always walked alone. I walked alone with God as a child, independently, separately from my mother and the rest of my family. Sundays brought light into my dark world.

It was 1972, and I was twelve years old.

Walking alone didn't seem much different than walking with my mother. I have always walked alone, I realized, not for the first time. And the same familiar heavy feeling accompanied me; it felt as if I carried a full backpack.

My thoughts, a twisted jumble of memories surfaced as my feet carried me along the well-known route. I remembered what my father had recently told me.

"I think you should be a Playboy bunny." I guess you do, I inwardly sneered. You apparently don't care if I see the dirty pictures in the stuff you leave around the house.

It was wrong, that I knew, and it made me feel dirty. And that wasn't all that made me feel that way. The contradiction between my turbulent and obscure home life and the clear light that church portrayed was too great, and my spirit knew it. I felt overwhelmed by the guilt and shame imposed on me. I was caught in the hypocrisy of the religion and the culture and my life at that time.

As was my custom, I walked along the street on the opposite side from the church. Getting close, I again noted the building's beauty and recognized the purity it represented—a sharp contrast to my feelings and experiences.

My invisible backpack stayed with me; it remained full of my thoughts, pain, and memories … my burdens. I felt sad, unworthy.

I chose to walk on the opposite side of the street from the church, looking at the church the entire time until I crossed over. In my heart, God was real, and His Spirit was with me, and I understood and felt my family's hypocrisy.

Yet every week as I walked past, I admired the beauty of the light-colored brick church. To this day, I have not seen another as beautiful. The church itself was octagon-shaped, the shape signifying transformation, often used in baptismal fonts.

I am not the one doing these things, I thought. Why does it feel as if their acts are my own? Can I really walk into this church carrying all this with me? Do I—can I—really have a relationship with God?

Crossing the street, then walking into the church, brought my thoughts and emotions to a halt, and I could focus on God. Inside, the light blue interior enveloped me, and I felt as if the sky was all around me. I walked up the center aisle to my seat.

Here, for now, I felt good. I put my invisible backpack down and started participating in what was happening around me. I felt wonderful.

• CHAPTER 2 •

Longing for Relationship

Never will I leave you; never will I forsake you.

—Hebrews 13:5 NIV

UNTIL I WAS FIFTEEN, the familiar route to church became a haven of sorts. The sense of feeling unwanted, a nuisance and unloved by my mother, combined with the sometimes violent fighting between my parents and my father and brother, and memories of other paralyzing acts, always lurked close by, like an unwanted but always expected guest.

But Sunday.... Sunday remained my safe haven for a time.

Back and forth, my feet took me to St. Claire's. The nuns there told us that if we prayed the rosary on the way to church, we could sit in the front with them during Mass. That's what I did.

Hail Mary, full of grace, the Lord is with you.... I prayed the words Gabriel greeted Mary with when he told her she was to become the mother of Jesus while I walked the familiar route. Sometimes I stopped by the Italian bakery for bread or a pastry along the way.

I knew how to pray the rosary; I knew the prayers, but I don't remember making a prayer commitment. Still, it was a very spiritual experience for me. I felt close to God, and I wanted to be close to God.

> *And blessed is the fruit of your womb, Jesus....*
>
> *Our Father who art in heaven, hallowed be Thy name....*

When I arrived at church, I would find an open spot to sit in the first rows with the nuns. I listened intently during the priest's homily, and sometimes I had questions, so I asked them—right then. Though this was probably not the ideal place to ask questions, I genuinely wanted answers. The priest, instead of answering, would shake his finger at me. Eventually, the nuns told me I had to be quiet, or I couldn't sit there anymore.

I knew my Sunday experience was over. My walks to the church would end. I would put down all I had clung to so tightly all those years. All that kept me safe was coming to an end, and I didn't understand why.

Finally, one day, the feeling was overwhelming (a feeling I would again experience more than a decade later). I knew I simply couldn't continue. I walked to St. Claire's for the last time, holding tightly to my rosary beads. This time, however, I wasn't praying. I knew I had to obey the leading of the Spirit, the sense that I needed to walk away from the church that had been my refuge. Why? I don't want to, I groaned deeply; but I wanted to obey, and I did.

I knew I had to obey the leading of the Spirit, the sense that I needed to walk away from the church that had been my refuge.

That next Sunday I walked right into the church. I was nervous about meeting the nuns who knew me, but no one was there. I did not genuflect as I normally did. I did not cross myself with holy water. No, I stood in the back of the church, knowing this was not the place God wanted me to be any longer. I did not understand why; I had always loved going to church.

I walked down the center aisle of the church, making a left turn down a smaller aisle where the statue of Mary stood. My hands were sweaty from holding the rosary so tightly, and when I opened my hand, the impression of the beads was in my palm.

I laid my rosary at Mary's feet.

"I can't do this anymore," I said, and I wept.

Today, I understand that God the Father, through the power of His Spirit, was calling me into a personal relationship with Jesus Christ His Son. At the time, I remember feeling that I had done something right. In fact, that was a starting point in my search for a genuine relationship with God. To do so, I rebelled against the faith I was born into, but with the intention of having a better relationship with God, to find God and know His plan for me.

It was 1975, and I was fifteen.

I'm not sure my parents even noticed. One Sunday, my mother asked me to stop by the bakery to pick up bread. "I'm not going to church today," I responded. Nothing else was said.

Even as a young child, I knew I wanted a relationship with God. In fact, without really knowing it, my search for God was essentially a search for my Savior. As an adult, I know that before you realize you need a Savior, you need to understand that you are lost and unable to save yourself.

For three years, I walked alone to church.

Three years later, I would walk away from my family as well.

• CHAPTER 3 •

Childhood Trauma

EVEN AS A CHILD, I knew God was always with me. As I lay in bed, crying and shaking from fear, listening to the cursing, yelling, and uncomfortable conversation outside my room, I prayed, God, *if you take me today, I will have everything I need.* I prayed to God as a young child, clutching my teddy bear and blanket in my bed.

But we need much more than our pillow, and blanket, and a teddy bear to be with Him. I came to realize that what I needed was a relationship with Him to save me, heal me, and forgive me from and for what I was about to experience.

I remember it very well. I was three years old....

Feeling ashamed and dirty, I looked down at the impression our rag rug made on my skin. I had played with my dolls there while my parents were out for so long that the imprint remained.

I couldn't speak out. I had been warned.

What started there became the seeds of a recurring nightmare … one of a giant black snake. Up the stairs it slithered, from the basement all the way to my third-floor bedroom. The dream recurred for a while, then stopped until my senior year in high school.

As an adult, many years later, I saw the movie *Anaconda*, and I got physically sick because it reminded me of the dream. To me, the dream represented the anxiety, stress, and abuse. I felt as if there was a powerful force that was trying to harm me, and I always felt I had to be on guard because of this dream, even when I was awake.

My brother started getting into trouble and would fight with my father. My father could be violent and often hit him. Sometimes, my brother would get in trouble and disappear for a couple of days, and when he returned home, dad would beat him again.

All the while, I was going to church with my mom and praying about what was happening. At the same time, I locked away the abuse in some compartment in the back of my mind and heart. I didn't tell anyone about the abuse while it was going on. I didn't even talk to God about it. I didn't know I could.

After my brother graduated from high school, he joined the army, but was diagnosed with ulcerative colitis and got out early on a medical discharge. When I was fourteen, he moved back home for a couple years, even though my father didn't want him to live at home again.

During my junior year in high school, my father finally threw him out of the house.

Impact of Childhood Trauma

What early childhood abuse does to the mind impacts future decisions, and therefore life as an adolescent and adult can be bleak and desolate without a person knowing why. The symptoms can include passive-aggression, victimhood, presenting a false front, depression, anxiety, and addiction. Descriptions of these symptoms are taken from an article posted by The Treatment Specialist. (See Appendix A.)

Knowing God, prayer, and fellowship with believers are very important and they were key for my healing.

I was turning 18. I was getting ready to graduate from high school and trying to plan my future. At the time, my parents showed no interest or desire to help me go to college. I wanted to be a veterinarian, and it was required that a parent take me. My mom took me to pre-graduation counseling where they went over what veterinary school would entail and how much it would cost. Later at home, my mom and dad told me that if I wanted to go to veterinary school, I would have to do it myself; they refused to help.

Why don't they encourage me to go to college? I wondered. But one didn't question my father.

My hurt grew to anger, then to fury.

Then I became resentful. I was disappointed in them, and I internalized it for a while. I simply couldn't understand why they didn't encourage me to go to college and hadn't made any provision for it. I guess it just wasn't a priority for them, so I assumed they came out of a culture that was mostly uneducated and they didn't value getting an education.

Ultimately, their refusal to help became the final "straw." I erupted and told them about the abuse I suffered. I'm not sure how I expected my parents to react, but my revelation quickly turned into a heated argument. My mom didn't believe me and said I was making up the story. Even today, I still don't know if she really thought I was lying, or she was simply denying it had happened. My mother's disbelief, combined with their unwillingness to help me go to school, was the fuel I needed to pack up whatever I could carry and leave home the day after I graduated high school.

It was 1978 … on my eighteenth birthday.

I packed up what I could carry—literally—and left for the train. Then, not sure what I should do, I called Leigh.

Years before, sitting on the train on my way to work after school, a young man approached me.

"Hi," he said. "I really like that dress."

"Thanks, I created it myself."

We sat together and talked until I got off the train at my stop and entered the restaurant where I worked as a waitress.

During high school, beginning at fourteen, my parents strongly encouraged me to work, so I found a job working as a waitress in a diner not far from my house. Every afternoon, I rode the train to work after school and worked there until eight o'clock. I did that for three years. On the train, I met Leigh, and we became friends. As I got closer to graduation, we started to date. Leigh was six years older than I.

As I began to have a more intimate relationship with him, I began to share some of the trouble I was having at home. At the beginning of my senior year of high school, I began to have the dream about the snake again. It frightened me because I hadn't thought about the abuse for a while; it remained in the compartment where I had put it away, years before.

Leigh knew I planned to leave home after graduation, but I didn't plan it to happen this way. Leigh was Jewish and an aspiring musician. He played the bongos and loved to smoke pot and listen to the Grateful Dead. He liked to take long walks in the woods and commune with nature. He was a very sweet, timid, caring person, and I genuinely cared for him.

The whole argument with my parents was passionate, occurring in the anger of the moment. It was too much. I didn't plan to leave beforehand, and I didn't plan to call Leigh. It just happened. I needed to get away from the violence in my parents' house.

As I left, I stopped under the cherry tree my father planted for my mother in the front yard of the house we moved into when I was in middle school. The tree was in bloom and the wind was blowing the blossoms away. A change of season was coming for me also. I breathed it in and watched as the wind caught the blossoms and took them afar. It looked and felt like pink snow falling upon, surrounding, and moving me forward. Then I started to walk toward the train, alone,

It looked and felt like pink snow falling upon, surrounding, and moving me forward. Then I started to walk toward the train, alone, not really sure what I should do at that moment.

not really sure what I should do at that moment. And I called Leigh.

He met me at the Staten Island Ferry terminal and from there took the ferry into Manhattan and just walked around with all my stuff. At that time, I was an artist. I loved to paint. With me I had a canvas tied to my back, my artist box, my suitcase, and my teddy—my little panda bear. We walked onto the car level on the ferry and stood between the cars. He gave me a kiss and said, "This is going to be fun."

Then we lit up a joint.

We got off the ferry in Manhattan and walked around Liberty Park a little while. He started to play his bongo. He had a little box he carried with him all the time, so he sat down and played his bongo, and got some money. Then we got something to eat, and he called his sister who lived in Jersey City. She said we could come there. We took the subway from lower Manhattan to Jersey City, and we ended up staying with her a month or so.

Though I didn't think so at the time, Leigh was my escape from my parents' house. I'm sure our relationship gave me a sense of security I wouldn't have had otherwise.

• CHAPTER 4 •

New Beginnings

THANKFULLY, I QUICKLY FOUND a job working in an insurance company dining room in New York City, and Leigh began to look for work as a musician. Employees there were allowed to take leftovers home, and I took as much as I could carry.

Not too much time passed before we moved into an old gothic-style four-story house in St. George, on Staten Island. The house looked like it came from the movie *Psycho*, and we lived on the top floor. We had a magnificent view of the New York downtown skyline. Though we had nothing else, we had that view.

We placed plywood in the seats of two old café chairs we found in the neighborhood trash, so we could sit on them. We slept on a mattress on the floor. It's a good thing we lived on the fourth floor, because we didn't have curtains.

Walking home from the ferry was an uphill journey. One day, I was very upset, not sure what I was doing or where I was going. A tiny black kitten jumped out and began to follow me. For a moment I forgot about my sense of melancholy and turned my attention to "Raisin." She was all black like a raisin, so I named her and claimed her. She slept with me, washed with me, and was the best alarm clock. She, like me, loved to sit on the ledge looking out at the Manhattan skyline, or perhaps the trees that surrounded the house on the lower floors. I loved my little Raisin, but one day she was gone, and so was my joy.

Leigh looked for work but had a hard time finding gigs. But he did play music in our apartment. We had huge windows that opened, and there was a wide ledge, wide enough to sit on, so he would play music as we sat out there on the ledge under the stars, admiring the Manhattan skyline.

Often, the two of us would go into Manhattan to walk around, and Leigh and I would go into clubs so he could inquire about work. Sometimes, he would sit on a corner and play to make some money. Like many aspiring musicians, he ended up taking another job. He found a job working for an insurance company, and he was miserable about it.

After a while, I told Leigh I felt uncomfortable about living together. He was so gentle; he would not want to offend me. Then, more than once, he asked, "Why don't we just go there?"

"Well, are you proposing to me?" I responded. He chuckled about that a little bit. And I said, "Well, I think that that would be the best thing for us to do. Yeah. We should get married and just make it right."

Leigh and I were married in downtown Manhattan at City Hall. No one came. We invited my mother and father, but they did not come. We invited his mother and his step-father, but they couldn't be there. Someone from city hall stood with us as witness, and we had no one else.

On our wedding day, I wore the purple dress Leigh commented on the day we first met on the train, with a pair of beautiful sequined Oriental slippers from Hong Kong that Leigh asked his mother to bring back for me. He gave them to me as a wedding gift, but we never had rings.

Afterward, we just went home. We married because it was the right thing to do.

For me, this was the beginning of a new chapter in my life, and though it was full of uncertainty, the unknown, it was rather exciting. I was walking away from Catholicism and all I had loved and believed. Leigh was Jewish and stepping into a Jewish world was thrilling. As someone who had been trying to find God, I now had the opportunity to explore this God of the Jews.

I learned about the Jewish culture from Leigh's family. His mother was not a traditional Jew. She celebrated Passover, but she didn't frequent the synagogue. Leigh and I would celebrate the Sabbath with his mother; I often helped her with the meal. I remember eating my first parsnip at her house. Sometimes I prepared the meal myself—a Jewish meal with Italian flair.

Leigh's grandmother was a wonderful woman. She was little, at four feet eleven inches tall, and she wore glasses like jelly jars, so her eyes were three times as big. She spoke absolutely no English, and she lived alone in a two-room apartment on the first floor. And she was just a sweetheart. I remember walking to her apartment from the train station and her kitchen window was right next to the door of the apartment building. She had the window open, and the curtain was blowing. So, I used to move the curtain over to say, "Hello, I'm here." And she would motion, "Come, come, come." The first thing we would do was eat, which is very much like the Italians, so I felt very comfortable.

The first egg cream I had, she made for me. Egg cream is simply chocolate syrup and seltzer, but to this day hers is the best I've ever tasted. The first time I ate with her, I asked for butter for my bread, and I thought she was going to have a heart attack—the kosher rule is you don't mix meat and milk, and the sandwich was beef salami.

I became very interested in the Jewish faith and started to read books on Judaism. I had the idea that this was God's plan all along—for me to be Jewish. About two years into my relationship with Leigh, I began to investigate how to become a Jew and was astonished to learn that you can't. You can follow Judaism, but you can't become a Jew—the Jews are the "chosen people."

To be chosen sometimes is a great honor, but it can also be an extremely difficult position to be in. And when you are chosen by God to do something, a particular task, there is no guarantee there will be a reward or recognition. For the chosen people, while they were in the wilderness, being chosen meant eating manna and wearing the same clothes for forty years (Ex. 16.4; Deut. 29:5).

They lived under a flame at night and a cloud by day, which was there to give them direction. It was only after much suffering and confusion that God allowed His chosen people to realize what they were chosen for.

Now I understand that God was calling me out of the dark, the legalism of an organized religion. Being a child of God is about relationship, not religion; it's about a relationship with the Creator of the world.

While I didn't understand the concept of spirituality as a child, I did understand belief in God for His purpose. We are all born with a purpose, Scripture tells us. John the Baptist was given a purpose before he was born (Luke 1:13-17). First Peter 2:9 says, "But you are a chosen people, a royal priesthood, a holy nation, God's special possession, that you may declare the praises of him who called you out of darkness into his wonderful light" (NIV). Ephesians 2:10 reads, "For we are God's handiwork, created in Christ Jesus to do good works, which God prepared in advance for us to do" (NIV).

God calls us out of the dark for His purpose—not just for our salvation, but also to proclaim His glory, power, strength, and wisdom.

God calls us out of the dark for His purpose—not just for our salvation, but also to proclaim His glory, power, strength, and wisdom. Most of the time, we act as if we are in control of our lives, and we simply don't realize that God is there. He is there through everything we do and encounter. He was with me as a child, with all I endured. He was with me through my fight with my parents and moving in with Leigh. And He remained with me through what was to come. In fact, He was preparing me to be where I needed to be twenty years later.

He was preparing me to be right here, now, sharing my experience to help others—to help you, potentially, to avoid the lies, the pain, the lifetime of hurt that often accompanies the circumstances I endured, and the choices I made.

• CHAPTER 5 •

Pain and Lasting Grief

THE YEAR WAS 1981—THREE years after my phone call to Leigh—and I was pregnant and thrilled out of my skin. But a hiatal hernia that began as a child returned with full force. Pain intense enough to double me over would last for hours. Eventually, slowly, the pain would subside. At my first appointment with my gynecologist, I learned I would have this pain throughout my pregnancy, and not only that, but the pain would increase as the baby grew. Several weeks went by, and I still hadn't told either my parents or Leigh. The pain, though, kept getting worse. Eventually, the pain became so bad that I ended up in the hospital.

Lying there in that hospital bed, I felt more emotions at one time than I had ever felt: confusion about my illness and the accompanying pain; unsure why I was feeling so terrible when I was happy about being pregnant; love for the baby I was carrying; and the fear every young mother feels.

Much to my surprise, my mother walked into the room. She was alone. She had been notified that I was admitted to the hospital because I was still a dependent on my father's health insurance. Seeing her, I felt like a trapped mouse. The look on her face as she entered my hospital room was a look I knew well—a look like she was ready to blow up the world. Her first words to me, in a torrent of breath, were, "You can't have this baby."

Her words stabbed my heart.

In the end, the doctors, the nurses, and my mother all offered no choice but to have an abortion. Actually, my mom insisted. The doctor encouraged it, and he squelched any hopes of my having a healthy child with medical terms I don't even remember. For good measure, the doctor threw in that I would only continue to have the pain that put me in the hospital in the first place. When I searched the nurse's face, I didn't find a trace of what I thought nurses should have: compassion.

The doctor's office made the appointment, and when the day came, I went alone to the Margaret Sanger Clinic in Manhattan. I was there overnight, and Leigh didn't know I was in the hospital. He still did not know I was pregnant, and I certainly hadn't told him I was about to kill his child.

The building where the clinic was located looked normal enough on the outside, but it was a brick killing chamber. It was not like the ones used during the Holocaust, reeking of death. This one had a pleasant aroma, but the results were the same.

The elevator door opened to an office buzzing with the sound of workers, nurses, doctors, and other victims, which is what I considered myself.

I was quickly taken to a holding room where the triage nurse told me not to worry, that in an hour or so my life would be back to normal. I had sunk into a chair thinking, *I want this baby, and I don't want to do this.* I wanted to find a way out and run as fast as I could. But at the clinic they had one objective—to complete the abortion. They offered no alternatives, no counseling, no guidance, and no comfort. The triage nurse took me to a prep room where I allowed them to take my baby.

I could have argued with my mom. I could have shouted at the doctor to shut up. And although I felt like spitting in the nurse's face, I didn't. Had I been counseled about the effects of abortion, I might have known the facts and found the courage to change my mind. If my heart had been right before God, I wouldn't have been in that situation. I would have kept my baby despite what anyone said. If I was told that years after the experience of that day, I would suffer from post-abortive stress syndrome (PASS), a form of post-traumatic stress disorder (PTSD), I would have made a different choice. But now, I still suffer from the choice I made, like many other men and women. We suffer in silence!

Had I been counseled about the effects of abortion, I might have known the facts and found the courage to change my mind.

If I had known the words from Ephesians 3 all those years ago, I believe I would have had the strength to resist the choice to go through with abortion. Today, this verse gives me the courage to reveal the horrible lies, the pain, and the relentless frustration that comes from making that choice. God is able by His power to do more than we can ask. He is at work in our lives, and when we allow Him, He will use us for His glory in a way that we do not give in to the pressure put on us from the world's point of view.

> **Now to him who is able to do immeasurably more than all we ask or imagine, according to his power that is at work within us, to him be glory in the church and in Christ Jesus throughout all generations, forever and ever! Amen.**
>
> —Ephesians 3:20–23 NIV

• CHAPTER 6 •

Out on the Ledge

Then the man and his wife heard the sound of the LORD God as he was walking in the garden in the cool of the day, and they hid from the LORD God among the trees of the garden.

—Genesis 3:8 NIV

WHEN THE CLINIC ALLOWED me to leave, I went home and was sick, physically sick. I escaped onto the ledge, to the place where I internalized all my feelings. At that moment, I wish I had known how to pray to the Lord, or even that I could pray. Instead, I hid on the ledge. In Genesis 3:8, Adam and Eve tried to hide themselves from God. That's what I was attempting to do. But as was proven to Adam and Eve, you cannot run from or hide from God.

Why? I asked myself. *Why did I allow this?* What I did was intentional … deliberate. I felt no better than a person who held a knife to someone's throat or a gun to their head. I had killed my child, and I felt I was at the darkest point of my life.

I did not feel in touch with reality. The view from the ledge that always brought peace and happiness was not there. I couldn't see beyond what I did, what I had felt forced to do. A woman should be able to go to her mother for security, but my mother helped me arrive at this dark place.

I didn't even think of God. But one thought did echo in my mind: *Guilty as charged*. That same thought was on replay. *Murder in the first degree.*

Leigh had no idea what I had just done, and it was days before I could utter those words. When I did tell him, I could see the hurt in his eyes. I always felt guilty about not telling him. After all, it was his baby too.

Eventually, a few months after the abortion, we moved from our St. George sanctuary to Brooklyn, and things started to fall apart. One day we took the train from New York City home to Brooklyn. We both worked in the city, so we would meet and take the train back home to Brooklyn together, and we had quite a walk from the train to our apartment. We were arguing during the entire walk, and a woman walking on the other side of the street, wearing a jacket and hat that resembled the Salvation Army uniform, walked across the street and said to me, "Come with me, honey." I pushed her hand away. "Okay," she said, "just stop arguing."

Everything started to unravel from there. Now I believe it was the abortion. After that, all the choices we made were wrong or bad, like dominoes falling.

As I recall us splitting up, I think about how abortion not only affects the child and the mother, but the father as well. I can't imagine what Leigh must have felt when I told him about the abortion. I never gave him the opportunity to feel the joy or the fear of expecting a child. I robbed him of all those expectations of being a father. I think he would have made a wonderful father because he was a very gentle person. He was so gentle that he didn't even retaliate after I explained what had happened, but I knew I broke his heart by not discussing it with him, by taking matters into my own hands and letting others decide for me. It is so important for a woman to realize that when she becomes pregnant it is not just about her and her body, it is also about the father. It's a bond that can

It is so important for a woman to realize that when she becomes pregnant it is not just about her and her body, it is also about the father.

never be replicated in anyone else but his child. Whether good or bad, it is a one-of-a-kind bond—and I had selfishly taken it away.

I started distancing myself from him, and eventually we were divorced.

Wisdom does come with age, and over time I've learned that sexual abuse creates a heightened sense of sexuality. I used Leigh somewhat, though it was unintentional; I didn't know that at the time. I used him to leave home; he was exotic to a nineteen-year-old. I found him intriguing and handsome. He was six years older than I was, not my peer, not even a college student, and I had just graduated high school.

Leigh was a challenge, and I liked that. I liked the fact that he liked me. It was invigorating that an older man liked me. I've come to learn that this is actually a victim mentality.

Eventually, I left Leigh and returned to my parents' home. The last time I saw Leigh was when my father and I stopped by to give him divorce papers. I couldn't face him and asked my dad to go to the door for me. Leigh opened the door to my father's knock. That was the last time I ever saw him—from inside the car as my father served him the papers. I cried on the way back to my parents' home.

I know I hurt him, and I tried to locate him later, but I never found him. He deserved better.

My search for God began to permeate every part of my life, and it was through my search that I realized that God was not calling me to become a Jew. I knew it was not God who was leading me in that direction because the path led to a dead end. This realization, but mainly the abortion, caused a significant change in my relationship with Leigh, and it led to our marriage dissolving.

All the while I felt that I was running toward God, but He seemed to be getting farther away. However, I did not give up my pursuit. It almost became an obsession.

• CHAPTER 7 •

Motivated to Help

MY MOM ALLOWED ME to move back in. I lived in an apartment they had. Now back in my parents' home, I needed to figure out what to do with my life. Veterinary school was a thing of the past. Three years had passed, and I didn't want to relive the bad memories I tried to run away from.

After leaving Leigh, I started to sketch a lot. Once I sketched a ballerina I titled "Dance before Jesus" based on the song by the same name. I could sing the song in my head, and I had a vision of Jesus sitting in a chair, a high-backed chair. The sketch was from behind Jesus, so you could see the ballerina. And she was at His right hand, the best place to be … God's right hand. Looking at the sketch, His right hand is on the arm of the chair, and the ballerina is in third position, which is like a bow. She's in front of Him and bowing.

Through I wasn't born again, I had knowledge, like I was in tune with Him. As I look back, I understand I was seeking Jesus, even in those days. Like the wise men. They were learned men, and I'm not comparing my intelligence to theirs. They had knowledge that the king of the Jews had been born, and they were seeking Him from afar. They were seeking this King who today we know is the King of all mankind. Though they weren't Jews—they were from Persia, India, and Arabia—different, outsiders like me—they saw His star and wanted to worship Him (Matt. 2:2).

I knew from my position in the insurance company dining room that I enjoyed cooking and working in restaurants, and I wanted to do more in the food service and hospitality business. I continued to work as a waitress and started taking hotel and restaurant management classes at Brooklyn Technical College during the day. Then at night—from eleven at night to seven in the morning—I worked in a diner on Staten Island. Here I met my second husband, Nazir, a little more than a year after I left Leigh.

It was 1983. Nazir and I both worked in the diner, but while I was born and raised on Staten Island, Nazir was from Egypt. In my eyes, he was interesting and a little exotic. We both worked the graveyard shift.

Nazir pursued me. I resisted him at first, but eventually we went out. On our first date we went to a concert in Brooklyn featuring a famous Egyptian vocalist named Wa'rda. I didn't like the music at all, but I liked the mystery I found in the strange music and the foreign language.

When I met Nazir, he told me he was divorced. Later, I found out he was still married and had a daughter in Egypt. I also eventually learned he was an illegal immigrant, but to his credit, he never asked me to marry him to get his green card—at least, that's what I thought at the time.

I was living in my mother's house when he asked me to marry him. My mother gave me permission to have the wedding in the house. Because we were of different faiths, getting married in a church was out of the question. No family members were invited; that would be too shameful. Just a handful of friends and my parents were present.

It was December, and I wanted lots of poinsettia plants. I made a ring of them around the Christmas tree, which we stood in front of as a non-denominational clergyman officiated. We were married on Saturday and went back to work on Monday. I never completed my degree in Restaurant Hotel Management, and I left the job at the diner late that winter to work in a real estate office. I missed the city. My new workplace was located in the Upper West Side, right off of Central Park West—a beautiful, sycamore tree-lined street that ran right into the Hudson River. Muddy as it was, it was still beautiful. I often got off the subway a stop early to walk a bit. I liked walking between the tall stone buildings. I especially loved how warm the buildings felt to the touch as the sun left its mark on them. The shadows of the pigeons perched on the ledge would dot the buildings, like polka dots. The buildings reminded me of the Bible stories I had read. I also remembered reading in the Bible that when Jesus returned, not one stone would remain atop another.

> **And Jesus said to them, "Do you not see all these things? Assuredly, I say to you, not one stone shall be left here upon another, that shall not be thrown down."**
>
> —Matthew 24:2 NKJV

Thinking I could escape the collapse of one of those buildings, I ran to the corner, pushed the traffic signal button, and waited to cross to the park where I felt safe. I loved walking past Central Park—the musicians lined the sidewalks with their open boxes asking to be filled with spare change. I often stopped at a small coffee shop near my office for breakfast.

I never thought about the homeless or a homeless ministry. I saw them as part of the landscape of the city. One day, though, I noticed a woman dressed entirely in black. Everything she wore was black. She was old … standing in the doorway of the storefront next to the coffee shop. It was as if she was deliberately planted there for me to notice her. She didn't look at me—she looked into me, and I couldn't forget her. I looked for her during my lunch break, but she wasn't there. That was on Friday. That was the first time I truly noticed a homeless person.

She didn't look at me—she looked into me, and I couldn't forget her.

On Monday, my first stop was to find that woman. As I turned the corner of Central Park West onto 72nd Street, there she was, this time walking, almost pacing, back and forth in front of the coffee shop. I stopped in her path.

"Hello," I said. "Can I buy you a sandwich?"

Again, she looked into me.

"Yes," she responded.

From then on, I looked for her each day. Some days, I brought her food from home, and on other days I bought her something from the coffee shop. Time passed, and the weather was getting warmer. I noticed that she smelled very bad. My office was a Brownstone apartment equipped with a full bathroom. I asked her if she could meet me earlier the next day. The next morning, I met her at seven and walked with her to the Brownstone I worked in. I escorted her up the stairs and into the office, where I offered her clean clothes and showed her the bathroom. I heard the water turn on and sounds of relief—like music—coming through the door.

All the while, my heart was pounding with fear from the thought of my employer coming in early and—well, I could only imagine her response.

"Can you please hurry?" I asked her. Then I wrapped her old clothes in a bag and returned them to her as I walked with her out of my office and down the stairs.

"Can I take you to lunch?" I asked as we left the building. "By the way, what's your name?"

"Dianah," she said.

I quickly returned to the office and cleaned the bathroom, removing any trace of the deed. All morning I thought about Dianah. When we met during my lunch break, she thanked me. Then she handed me a yellow file folder. Inside was a drawing she made, signed "Dianah." It was a black and white pencil drawing, very geometric. She wanted me to have it, a gift for my kindness, she said. That was Friday; I never saw Dianah again.

> **Do not forget to entertain strangers, for by so doing some have unwittingly entertained angels.**
>
> —Hebrews 13:2 NKJV

As I look back, I believe my experience with Dianah was a God moment. It was the starting place in my ministry working with the homeless, which would begin twenty-five years later. It planted a seed of compassion like no other.

I believe God was revealing something to me through a relationship with a Muslim.

Nazir and I settled into married life. After our marriage, I almost felt privileged to be able to provide residency status for him. His Muslim faith fascinated me, just as Leigh's Jewish faith had. There was, to me, something interesting and intriguing about Islam.

As before with Leigh, I believe God was revealing something to me through a relationship with a Muslim. I believe God allowed me to have the relationship with Nazir, even though it would later become traumatic. Still, the relationship and the familiarity I developed with the Muslim faith has given me a heart for people in the Middle East, and I continue to fan the flame.

Looking back, I believe Nazir stole a big part of my life from me. He lied to me about everything—everything. He lied about not being married. He lied about his daughter, Rhana. He told me about her eighteen months into our relationship. He insisted his relationship with his wife was over and he wanted to stay with me. However, I asked him to leave the house, and he did. It was the first of many times he would leave—but on subsequent occasions, he would abandon not only me, but his children as well. Nazir told me that while he was in Egypt, he had an affair with his ex-wife.

While we were separated, his wife called me from Egypt, where she was living with family. She had called me to curse me, and I apologized to her for being a part of the reason her life was difficult. I told her it never should have happened, that I didn't know about her and her daughter, and told her she could have him back. She told me she didn't want him.

With that being the case, I took him back, and we settled into married life again. I had always talked about getting pregnant, wanting to have a family with him, but he didn't seem to share the same joy when we talked about having a child. It was something we didn't share.

We seemed to be going in different directions. I wanted to build a family, but I had no idea what he was thinking. We were married, and I thought having a child was part of it. After learning I was pregnant, I was scared to tell him. His answer at the time was that he wasn't working steadily, and he felt he was going to be trapped or pressured in some way. I was afraid this would cause me to lose him, just as I had lost Leigh. I had an abortion for the second time in my life.

I guess you could say that it's ironic that having an abortion led to the breakup of my first marriage, and yet I decided to have a second abortion to try to save my second marriage.

• CHAPTER 8 •

Sweet Perfume

I FELT EMPTY, COMPLETELY empty, lost, and sick. I didn't know why. My actions were robotic, mechanical. As I sat on the train on my way to the Margaret Sanger Clinic—again—a woman wearing heavy, sweet-smelling perfume got on the train, and the aroma overwhelmed me.

Immediately, the smell combined with pregnancy made me nauseous. I had to get up and walk down the aisle of the train. After I passed her, I turned back to look for her … but she was gone.

Wait, I thought. *You can't just get off a moving train.*

It wasn't the Manhattan subway where you can transfer between cars internally. She was just … gone.

I sat back down and immediately remembered the scripture that God was a sweet, fragrant aroma, and I knew, I sensed, that God was with me on that train (Eph. 5:2). I still don't know why I went through with the abortion. I felt so lost. I think the Lord was still pursuing me and leading me to Himself.

All during the train ride into Manhattan I remember saying to myself, over and over, "*I am doing this again. I am on my way to the Margaret Sanger Clinic AGAIN!*" I felt absolutely lost. The only thing that kept me focused was that I was choosing the abortion to save my relationship with Nazir. Why did I feel I had to do this to secure our relationship? Why did I allow the baby to become a bargaining tool, the ransom for our relationship? From reading Scripture, I know now it was because my security was not in God. "It is better to take refuge in the LORD than to trust in man" (Psa. 118:8). My security was misplaced—I was trusting what a man said rather than what God said.

God promises in Hebrews 13:5 to never leave nor forsake us. I wish I could have identified with that. The rationales women come up with for having an abortion will not prevent us from dealing with the trauma, pain, and guilt that comes afterward.

Some women and men rationalize having an abortion by saying, "It's not the right time," or "I'm still in school," or "I/we have no money to support a family." These are all circumstances that may change after you have the abortion, but the fact that your baby has been aborted is forever. There are consequences you will live with for the rest of your life. It is crucial to identify the underlying issue that leads to abortion. The issue is that our heart is not right before God. Obviously, my heart was not right. My mind still held the effects of childhood trauma.

Walking into the Margaret Sanger Clinic, everything appeared, smelled, and felt exactly the way I remembered it the first time. The carpet was the same. It was the same shiny glass death chamber that it was several years before. While riding up in the elevator, I thought of the grape jelly and the saltine crackers they would give me after the procedure was over.

Again, when I went into the preadmission room, no one explained the procedure, no one gave me any options, and no one discussed the possibility of regret and remorse, otherwise known as Post-Abortive Stress Syndrome. They just smiled, and again said things would be back to normal in a little while.

However, things would never be back to normal—not even now, thirty years later. "Normal" has become living each day with the reality of what I did. It didn't change or improve my life or my circumstances. I still have money problems, and after thirty years, I am still in school.

Nazir didn't insist I have an abortion, but he didn't stop me, and he certainly didn't come with me. I came home from the clinic and sat on the couch in pain, bleeding. I told him that having the abortion didn't seem right.

I was taken aback by his lack of encouragement, love, or compassion, which really frightened me. But I brushed it off as being a cultural difference. I was afraid to lose him, and for some strange reason, the fear of losing him was more consuming than the idea of killing my child.

I know other women feel the same way, but I hope my experience exposes the lie. *Aborting your baby will not secure a man's love!* Life will not become normal, and nothing will change. If someone loves you, they will stay close through anything.

Aborting your baby will not secure a man's love!

Thinking about my relationship with my mom and dad, my brother, with my first husband Leigh, then with Nazir, I believe I have always desired to have a pure, honest relationship with family or with someone. It wasn't until I met Jesus that I found the pure, honest relationship I searched for.

Jesus has been my love for so long now. Many times, when I thought I was going to die, He healed my body. Rather than putting demands on me, He has allowed me to experience being involved in ministry and has allowed me to share with others the truth about society's deceptions, especially the deception that shouts, "You will be happier if you are allowed to make a choice."

We are blessed with freedom of choice in all things. Choice is important, but if the seemingly inconsequential choices we make in our day-to-day lives don't make us happier, how can the much weightier choice to terminate the life of your baby make you happier? Aborting your baby will not make your life better. It never makes your life better. It won't change your relationship with your parents. It won't make it easier to go to school or have a job. I can tell every woman that aborting your baby will not make your husband or boyfriend love you or stay with you.

When things seem hopeless and there seems to be no other choice, think twice. When we choose life, God will make a way when there seems to be no way.

Women should also recognize that their womb is the house where their baby dwells and should be a safe place—a house of comfort, nourishment, safety, and love.

Unless the woman stops herself from going into that clinic, abortion clinics will not close. Only by focusing on a woman's heart, by helping her open her heart toward the baby and helping her develop a right relationship with God, will we stop abortion.

If this is where you are today, if you are feeling sad, sorry, ashamed, or alone, if you are feeling unloved or unlovable because of abuse, bad decisions, abortion, or anything else, there is still hope for you. If life has put you in a position where you think you have no way out, you need to know that God will make a way when there seems to be no way. I want *you* to hear what God has to say to *you* today:

> **Remember not the former things, nor consider the things of old. Behold, I am doing a new thing; now it springs forth, do you not perceive it? I will make a way in the wilderness and rivers in the desert.**
>
> —Isaiah 43:18–19

What is this new thing? You can become part of the pure bride of Christ. You are invited to a banquet—not just any banquet, but a special wedding, to the kingdom of God. Jesus explained with a parable in Matthew 22. Jesus said His kingdom "is like a king who prepared a wedding banquet for his son" (Matt. 22:2 NIV). The king sent his servants to those who had been invited to the banquet to tell them to come, but they didn't show up. So, he sent more servants, this time with a message: "Tell those who have been invited that dinner is ready. Only the best food and drink is good enough to celebrate my son's marriage. Come …

come celebrate with me. Come enjoy the wedding and the prepared feast" (Matt. 22:4 paraphrased).

Still, no guests arrived. They went on with their lives; they went home or off to work. Some of the servants were killed for bringing the invitation. So, the king decided that those he invited didn't deserve to come. Then he sent his servants to the street corners and everywhere to invite anyone they could find.

You can become part of the pure bride of Christ. You are invited to a banquet—not just any banquet, but a special wedding, to the kingdom of God.

And they went out. To the abortion clinics. To the dark alleys. To the jails. To anywhere people hide their pain. To where you are right now.

The most important choice you will make in life is to accept the invitation to the wedding feast of the Lamb. The guests are those who acknowledge Jesus as the Savior of their lives and believe by faith that He has saved them and forgiven their past, present, and future sins. Life with Him is the new thing God wants to do for you.

When you arrive, be wearing a wedding garment, the one sometimes depicted as the seamless tunic Jesus wore on the way to Calvary, the one the soldiers fought over after His death. The one that represents His righteousness. His sinlessness. Our wedding garment.

You are invited because of the Lamb of God's perfect, sinless self-sacrifice for you. Make the best choice you will ever make—to be His bride, purified by the righteousness He bestows upon you as a robe.

> **Many are invited, but few are chosen.**
>
> —Matthew 22:14 NIV

You, my friend, are chosen to attend the marriage supper of the Lamb, but come dressed and ready, having chosen grace through faith. If only I had known this at the time of all my poor choices! Jesus was calling me from my hiding place, but I couldn't yet see Him.

I went to the clinic again—a third time—like a lamb led to slaughter. My marriage was only getting worse, and Nazir's behavior was growing ever darker. This time I heard the baby vacuumed into the tube. I believed I would never be forgiven for this horrible act against my child. I wanted to die. I tried to kill myself by taking a bottle of pills, but it didn't work. I ended up in the hospital with a pump down my throat. I cried out within myself, "Stop! Please let me die! I don't deserve to live!"

But God had other plans for me. "For I know the plans I have for you, declares the LORD, plans for welfare and not for evil, to give you a future and a hope" (Jer. 29:11).

God was speaking to the children of Israel with a promise that, even though they would be in exile for seventy years, He had plans for them. Their lives had purpose. The same is true for you and me. God has a purpose for us that He planned long ago. As humans, we fail, falter, and fall off the path of His plan. But God keeps pursuing us until we choose Him. We are His treasure, and He will use everything in our lives so that His power will be exalted.

> **But we have this treasure in earthen vessels,**
> **that the excellency of the power may be of God,**
> **and not of us.**
>
> —2 Corinthians 4:7 KJV

• CHAPTER 9 •

Saving Grace

THREE YEARS AFTER NAZIR and I were married, in 1988, Gazelle, our first daughter, was born. When I discovered I was pregnant, I was so scared I was shaking on the way to see the doctor. I was determined to have this child … I wanted to have children; I wanted to be a mom even as a young girl. As a girl I dreamed about having eight children and giving them all names starting with the letter "J." I imagined having tea parties with my daughters.

When I told Nazir the news, I immediately told him, "I'm having this baby." We didn't talk about it anymore. Within the first couple weeks of the pregnancy, I started to have very bad, very *real*, dreams. In my dream, I was lying in bed sleeping, and sitting at the end of my bed was this very old man, who was naked and reaching towards me. I would wake up screaming.

One night I had this dream and again woke up screaming, and I ran into the living room where Nazir was studying.

"Didn't you hear me screaming?" I asked.

"No."

I told him about the old man at the end of the bed, but as I spoke, I realized that the root of the dream was my fear that Nazir would ask me to have another abortion. The dream was not the only time when I felt my pregnancy was at risk. When I went to the doctor for a follow-up appointment, the blood test showed extremely low levels of progesterone, which is a hormone that feeds the placenta and nourishes the baby. A slight decline in progesterone can have adverse effects on the baby or the mother. I had been so happy I was going to have a baby, but the lack of progesterone produces feelings of panic, stress, and even thoughts of suicide. I couldn't understand what I was going through, but after the doctor explained why I was feeling this way, I was comforted.

Due to the lack of progesterone, I had to take medication that cost a hundred dollars per week. Getting the money for the progesterone would be very difficult, and again, this was threatening the baby. In addition, we were living on Staten Island and the doctor was in Manhattan. I remember going on the ferry to the doctor at the end of six weeks of medication, and I saw the Statue of Liberty. I had seen it thousands of times, but this time I said, "You are such a big woman, a strong woman, representing power and strength." I felt so encouraged and empowered.

I had blood work and an exam done, and the doctor came out and called me into the consultation room and said everything is where it should be—the progesterone was good and I did not need to continue taking the expensive medication.

I left the doctor's office and was floating on air. I was so thrilled and happy, holding my stomach as I walked.

Nazir and I remained married for fifteen years, and during that time, our five children were born, but our marriage was tumultuous. After lying about being married and having a child, I found out he had a gambling problem. To top it off, he abandoned us time and again. But I loved Nazir. I loved being married. I loved the idea of being married.

Once on Christmas Eve, he left us again, when our second child, our son, was four. He was frantic, thinking his father was hurt.

Nazir continued gambling heavily throughout our marriage. Eventually, he gambled away one of our restaurants, and we lost the other. We faced foreclosures and evictions … and, on top of all that, he would leave whenever he chose. When he decided to leave, he didn't leave us money to survive on, so I would work a shift at one of our restaurants—before we lost them—then pay myself, so I could buy food and take care of essentials.

After we lost both restaurants, he went to work making pizza in a topless restaurant and bar in our neighborhood. One night after work, he came home, obviously high on something. He went to sleep on the floor in the living room and remained there throughout the next day—asleep. He remained asleep, even as the kids were stepping over him. I never mentioned it, but I'm sure they realized something was wrong.

At some point, after more than a decade of leaving and coming, of foreclosures and evictions, I asked the police how I could legally keep him from returning home. I discovered that if he left for thirty consecutive days, I could change the locks and block him from coming back into the house. So that's what I did. I got a calendar and started counting.

He would stay gone a week then return, a couple weeks then return. The first time he stayed gone thirty days, I took action. On the thirty-first day of his absence—at midnight—I packed the five kids into the car and we went to the police station.

Thirty-one is the number of chapters in Proverbs—I was growing wise.

"I'm here to let you know Nazir has been gone thirty-one days. If he comes back, I will not let him in."

He never did return. I waited for him to come back, and, truthfully, his absence broke my heart and the hearts of his children.

His leaving threw me immediately into foreclosure.

During the trauma of our daily life, God was there. Gazelle had a friend who was being confirmed and Gazelle wanted to be baptized. I met a Jehovah's Witness who began to connect me to an organized church. Along the way, God was navigating my journey. Closing one door and opening another. Shutting another door and opening a window. Severing this relationship and creating a new relationship … I felt like the ball in a pinball machine. I was trying to get to the right place. The bells and whistles were going off and I didn't know what I was doing.

Along the way, God was navigating my journey.

I was just following His star.

I always knew in my heart that God was there. I always had faith that He was there.

He was there in Dianah, in the lady on the train, when I cried out to Him early in my pregnancy with Anna, my fourth child, afraid she would be harmed by the radiation therapy I had undergone during treatment for Graves Disease. He gave me sweet sleep, then, upon waking, a deep peace, the peace that surpasses understanding, all within a few hours.

God was and is always with me—and you. Consider Hagar's story.

In Genesis 16, Hagar flees from Sarai because Sarai mistreated Hagar after she was pregnant with Abraham's child. God reveals Himself to Hagar in the desert and gives her a promise. Hagar gives God the name El Roi, "the God who sees." Hagar is the only person in the Bible who named God personally.

> **Now Sarai, Abram's wife, had borne him no children. But she had an Egyptian slave named Hagar; so she said to Abram, "The LORD has kept me from having children. Go, sleep with my slave; perhaps I can build a family through her."**
>
> **Abram agreed to what Sarai said. So, after Abram had been living in Canaan ten years, Sarai his wife took her Egyptian slave Hagar**

and gave her to her husband to be his wife. He slept with Hagar, and she conceived.

When she knew she was pregnant, she began to despise her mistress. Then Sarai said to Abram, "You are responsible for the wrong I am suffering. I put my slave in your arms, and now that she knows she is pregnant, she despises me. May the Lord judge between you and me."

"Your slave is in your hands," Abram said. "Do with her whatever you think best." Then Sarai mistreated Hagar; so, she fled from her.

The angel of the Lord found Hagar near a spring in the desert; it was the spring that is beside the road to Shur. And he said, "Hagar, slave of Sarai, where have you come from, and where are you going?"

"I'm running away from my mistress Sarai," she answered.

Then the angel of the Lord told her, "Go back to your mistress and submit to her." The angel added, "I will increase your descendants so much that they will be too numerous to count."

The angel of the LORD also said to her:

"You are now pregnant and you will give birth to a son. You shall name him Ishmael, for the LORD has heard of your misery. He will be a wild donkey of a man; his hand will be against everyone and everyone's hand against him, and he will live in hostility toward all his brothers."

She gave this name to the LORD who spoke to her: "You are the God who sees me," for she said, "I have now seen the One who sees me." That is why the well was called Beer Lahai Roi; it is still there, between Kadesh and Bered.

So Hagar bore Abram a son, and Abram gave the name Ishmael to the son she had borne. Abram was eighty-six years old when Hagar bore him Ishmael.

—Genesis 16:1-16 NIV

Just as God was with Hagar while she was on the run and had given up on life, He will be with you when you are at the end of your strength, hope, and ability to make wise decisions.

• CHAPTER 10 •

Making All Things New

I KNEW GOD HAD a plan for the mess of my life, to make a testimony for His glory; but how, when, and what would that look like?

My children and I enjoyed going to New York State during summer breaks. We mostly went to a Christian camp in the Adirondack region. The camp also offered a Bible college campus, which my children attended after graduating from high school. During summer break, I visited the camp to relax and enjoy the beautiful mountains and pine trees.

The trip to the camp was seven hours long. I often stayed overnight when I dropped the children off for school. My daughter's friend lived near the campus and her family welcomed me to stay the night before heading back to New Jersey the next day. I attended church with my host family that Sunday. As I sat in the back, the pastor's voice faded into the background of what God was saying and where He was leading me. The Spirit of God led me to read Genesis 22, where God tells Abraham to bind his son Isaac on the altar for a sacrifice.

"Okay God, you are telling me to sacrifice my children?" The call was strong and direct. I slammed my Bible shut so loudly that the people sitting nearby turned to see what the noise was. I left my seat and walked outside. *NOPE, I'm not causing them any more harm. I will do anything for You, but I can't, I won't, tell them about my past.*

Do you think I am unable to heal them from their pain, to restore them and your relationship?

God immediately impressed upon my mind, "Do you think I am unable to heal them from their pain, to restore them and your relationship?"

During a usual week of camp, I resolved to tell my children. Everything—all of it—needed to come out. I wanted God to use the mess of my life for good. To do this, my children needed to hear the story from me first. We loved a good camp fire, the stories, the songs, the memories we had made in the past. We always felt good around the campfire, so I decided that was a good time to talk to them, all together.

As I peeled off a layer at a time, I saw their faces, aglow from the campfire, fall from happiness to grief. I asked them to forgive me—the siblings they had never known, the silence I had lived in, the pain I had carried alone. My reflection included my memory of putting the children to bed, closing the bathroom door, and standing in front of the open window, looking up into the night and crying my eyes out, pouring my heart out—mourning my children gone, but not forgotten. It was a grief I could hardly bear.

The summer I told my children about my abusive past and the abortions, I told them I would speak to them individually or together about the circumstances. I hoped Gazelle would ask why I decided to keep her but not her siblings before her, but she never did. Gazelle, I believe, has always felt that I didn't love her as much as her siblings. I love all my children. But I wanted to tell Gazelle that I loved her so much that I was never going to allow anyone or anything to take her away from me.

I wanted to tell her that I saved her life, but twelve years later, she saved mine.

She was twelve years old, the age at which I was confirmed, and she was a middle school student working on a history project. They were studying socioeconomics, specifically the causes that place people in negative economic conditions. Gazelle, without asking my opinion, chose to study unwed mothers and asked to interview me. I agreed.

"Well, why don't we go and sit down and have some coffee or a donut?" I suggested.

We went to Dunkin' Donuts, and after we were seated, she asked: "What happened in your life that caused you to experience the difficulties you're having now?"

"I made mistakes when I was young. I left home too early. I allowed anger and fear to fuel my responses.... One thing led to another.... I didn't have the opportunity to go to college and do the things that would have made my life better."

I could sense His presence as if His arms were around me, and I was overwhelmed. I cried with release from knowing His presence, His love, and forgiveness.

Only short, quick, surface answers would come.

Suddenly, unexpectedly, I was overwhelmed with the past. Overwhelmed with pain and regret, ashamed of what I had done—all of it. Nauseous, I went to the bathroom and was sick—literally.

"Gazelle," I said when I could finally leave the bathroom and return to the table. "I don't feel well. We must go home."

The darkness, shame, and pain overwhelmed me. I knew I could not save myself from it. All the searching through all those years led me to this very moment of total surrender.

Later that night, I didn't feel any better. Right after everyone was in bed, I fell to my knees and lifted my arms to God. I cried out, *God, I cannot save myself. I cannot cleanse myself nor heal from the pain. Please forgive me for the abortions and the many other bad choices I made in my life. Please save me or take me!*

God poured a fountain of grace and mercy, like a flood of water, over me that night. I received Jesus Christ as my Lord and Savior, and His forgiveness has made me white as snow.

> **Purge me with hyssop, and I shall be clean;**
> **wash me, and I shall be whiter than snow.**
>
> —Psalm 51:7

God showed His love for me. I could sense His presence as if His arms were around me, and I was overwhelmed. I cried with release from knowing His presence, His love, and forgiveness. He saved me. Right then, He saved me.

In that moment, I identified with the sinful woman anointing the feet of Jesus with the costly oil. The cost of that oil, for me, was my children. My three children and the pain, shame, and the guilt I had carried all those years. That was the cost of the oil in my alabaster jar (Matt. 26:7).

God used my confession to Gazelle to help me recognize my need for a Savior.

That moment remains the turning point in my life. After that God encounter, that saving encounter, my life began to change. All the searching for all those years. All those bad decisions. First, I thought I was Catholic, then Jewish, then there was Nazir. In all of this, I was looking for God. I was looking, but He was right there all the time. I now know He was allowing me to experience the consequences of my own choices so that I would one day honor Him. When God saved me, He took all the pain, shame, and hurt away. He took it out of me. It was no longer festering inside me. He laid it all out on the table and said, "Yes, that was your life, but now you are forgiven and can be a living testimony of Me."

I was reminded of Moses (Ex. 2:11–15; 3:4). He murdered a man, fled from his home, and lived in a desert tending sheep alone. He had many years of isolation to think about what he had done and get right with God. Even with his past, God not only forgave him, but called him to deliver God's people from bondage. God uses broken people who respond to His purpose for their lives and seek restoration.

Life changed quickly. All the searching led me to the One who allowed me to find Him. By sharing my story, I pray that other women will come to know the God who created them—the God who loves them right where they are, regardless of what was done and how it happened. He is our forgiving and restoring God who loves those who seek Him.

CHAPTER 11

Elizabeth's Story

GOD HAS CREATED EVERY person unique, with DNA that is not identical to another's. With that come different personalities, looks, and responses to life. This is true of my children as well. Gazelle reacted one way to my story, Elizabeth another way. I did not realize how my story affected each one until I read Elizabeth's. I have included portions of it here, with her permission, to hopefully help others think about different personalities when telling their story and to tune in to their needs in the moment. Paul said in Philippians 2:3b-4: "In humility count others more significant than yourselves. Let each of you look not only to his

Being obedient to God often comes with a price, and we must prepare ourselves in advance through prayer and a listening ear to how the Lord is leading.

own interests, but also to the interests of others."

Being obedient to God often comes with a price, and we must prepare ourselves in advance through prayer and a listening ear to how the Lord is leading. Family secrets are a heavy load to carry alone, and unless the Lord leads us to share, we can know that He carries our burdens as we cast them at His feet. But when He does lead us to share, as He did me, we must understand that no matter how hard it is for ourselves and those who hear, it is for a purpose—to glorify God for the healing He has brought. As we prepare to be obedient to the Lord, it is critical to pray fervently for the ones with whom we will be sharing.

> **Cast your burden on the LORD,**
> **And he will sustain you.**
>
> —Psalm 55:22a

This promise from God is telling us that God will strengthen and support us physically and mentally as we give Him those things that trouble us. Those burdens we carry around like rocks in a backpack weigh us down, so we are unable to function properly. But when we take the backpack off and lay it down, the weight is lifted, and we are then able to stand straight and tall with the strength and support of God. Unless a person has experienced it, they cannot understand how it can be so, but it simply is as we trust by faith the promises of God.

Elizabeth's Story

Family meetings were common for us growing up. Emotions typically ran high in our household, and in that sense, having been asked to gather for what you can call a confessional felt normal. I felt the typical nerves, anxiety, and uncertainty, but again, this was somewhat typical.

As Mom started sharing, I felt like I was being given access to a story I had wanted to hear my entire life. Everything made sense after she finished speaking—everything.

"So, this is why we don't speak with that person; this is why Mom's relationship with her parents is so rocky; this is why Mom has only so much emotional stability; this is what all the secrets are." Those were my thoughts as I listened.

In addition to being told about Mom's abortions, we were also filled in on the fact that she had been sexually abused, as well as married to someone else prior to my dad.

Kids are incredibly observant, both emotionally and physically. If they are in a less-than-ideal situation, you can trust that they are noticing and feeling everything about it. So it is not fair to keep the pieces of the puzzle from them that will help them to understand and cope with the situation.

For a while, all children think about their parents is that they are simply parents. Young children only have the capacity to view themselves as the center and everyone else in relation. It is a very normal part of cognitive development. I believe healthy parent-child relationships are formed when the parent assists in the dissolution of that belief at age-appropriate times. I say this with no judgment, but my mother did not do that. She was so entrenched in the belief that her past was nothing but evil that she never shared more than the one side of her we knew—Mother.

To grow up not knowing anything about your parents, even though they are in your life, is a special kind of pain. Who is there to seek comfort from when things go wrong, when you mess up, when you have questions, and don't know your parents are also people who have messed up?

When Mom told me about the abortions, I felt angry that she had that life-changing choice robbed from her. I believe women need to be fully informed on all options so they alone can make the best choice for themselves and their families.

When she told me about the abuse she had suffered, I felt angry that people in her life did nothing to stop it. I felt anger that she had to face countless encounters with those who hurt her as if nothing had happened.

When she told me she was with someone significant to her before my dad, I felt angry I didn't know sooner. I felt angry that for my entire life, the family dynamics of my mother were kept from me. But in spite of it all, I was happy Mom had a time in her life so free and in love with someone, figuring out life together.

Kids deserve to know who their parents are. They deserve to know that good people make mistakes. They deserve evidence that goodness can follow pain. If not, when they are in places of mistakes and pain, they might feel like they are the first to go through it and there is not a way out. They might even think that life is supposed to be perfect, and it is their fault that it is not.

In answer to the question of my perception or opinion of Mom after she told us, it made me love her more. It made me want to know her more. It made me defensive of her faults and helped me see her in the most empathetic light possible because I finally knew what was causing all that pain.

Mom has a hard time letting people see any weaknesses she may have. I will never be happy she went through what she went through, but I am glad it opened the door for her children to relate to her in a more complete, sincere, and genuine light.

(I love you too, Elizabeth! —Mom)

• CHAPTER 12 •

Healing and Provision

SOON AFTER THE LORD set me free by His grace, I applied for a job at a church nursery, so I could bring my youngest daughter with me. At that church, I met Elizabeth (not to be confused with my daughter, Elizabeth), who became my spiritual mentor. Soon after I applied for the job, Elizabeth called me and said, "I'd like to invite you to come to a church meeting with us."

"Can I bring the kids?" I asked.

"Well, it would be better if you came by yourself."

I was able to find a babysitter, so I did go. The meeting was to pray for me.

Four people, Elizabeth, Perry, and two other women, laid hands on me and prayed for my healing. They prayed for me to be made whole and into what God intended for me before the foundation of the world.

All the words they said, all of them, made so much sense. It was what I was looking for all that time. I felt like

I had finally arrived. After the meeting, I went home feeling new. I just felt new. I felt born again, truly born again. Then a sequence of other events unfolded that reinforced their payers. My life has never been the same.

It was April 2000. My youngest daughter was born in 1999, and she was an infant. Nazir left for the last time in October that year, when she was only a few months old. When he left, I was immediately thrown into foreclosure, but God had other plans.

Not long after Nazir left, there was an unexpected knock at the front door. When I answered, I saw the sheriff, who was there to serve notice of foreclosure.

"How can I stop the process?" I asked him.

He stepped up onto one of the steps by my front door, which was odd. He came up close and said, "Go ask for a stay."

My children and I remained in that house for twenty-three years, though I was foreclosed on twice.

Another change in me was the time I spent in ministry and the Bible. God is the One who sees everything and knew everything I had done, what was happening, and loved me anyway.

God was calling me as He calls each of us, but He allows us to go on our way and make the mistakes we're going to make. Then He provides a way for us to come back. The calling is still there. He doesn't take it back just because we sin. There are no take-backs with God. The calling of God is irrevocable.

We're all broken, and God uses broken things.

About six years after Nazir left for good, the child support I had been receiving stopped. Working three jobs almost around the clock was not enough to keep the bills paid, so I began to fall behind in my monthly mortgage payments. It didn't take long before I was almost ten thousand dollars in arrears. I was faithfully attending a local Baptist church, serving on Wednesday evening with AWANA classes, and attending ladies' Bible study when it didn't conflict with my work schedule. It was there I shared my dilemma with a handful of ladies. I asked them to pray with me as I sought a solution. I received an official letter from the mortgage company regarding the late mortgage payments and their intent to begin foreclosure.

The ladies and I were going through the Book of Esther when I came across this.

> **And Mordecai told *them* to answer Esther: "Do not think in your heart that you will escape in the king's palace any more than all the other Jews. For if you remain completely silent at this time, relief and deliverance will arise for the Jews from another place, but you and**

> **your father's house will perish. Yet who knows whether you have come to the kingdom for** *such* **a time as this?"**
>
> **Then Esther told** *them* **to reply to Mordecai: "Go, gather all the Jews who are present in Shushan, and fast for me; neither eat nor drink for three days, night or day. My maids and I will fast likewise. And so, I will go to the king, which** *is* **against the law; and if I perish, I perish!"**
>
> —Esther 4:13–16 NKJV

I trust God and I trusted in the power of prayer to deliver me too!

During the next Bible study, I asked the ladies to pray with me *and* to fast as Esther did. For three days, no food, only water. Some of them were willing to join me in this.

Several weeks passed, and no relief was provided for my debt. I pulled into my driveway in tears after finishing a call with the mortgage company. "Until 4 p.m. tomorrow, that's it," the service rep had stated. Gripped with fear, I just cried.

Gazelle purchased an old car from a friend. It needed so much work just to run that I thought she was foolish spending her money on such a car. During church, prayer requests were always welcomed. Gazelle asked for assistance—a mechanic to help fix the car, for free she added!

As I sat in the car parked in the driveway, I tried to compose myself before going into the house. I noticed a man from church, Bill H., walking toward my car from the rear. I quickly dried my eyes as I greeted him. I rolled down the window and said, "Hi, what brings you here?" He noticed the pain on my face but did not question me about the tears that remained in my eyes. Instead, he reached into his shirt pocket and handed me a check. "This is from God—He loves you and so do I." I accepted the gift without knowing the amount on the check. I immediately felt reassured. Bill said, "I told Gazelle I was stopping by to help with her car and ... well I think you can figure the rest." The check was for $10,000, the amount I needed to satisfy the debt.

This is from God— He loves you and so do I.

He is the God who sees our need and provides in those times when we feel things are hopeless. God answered my prayers and delivered my family from another foreclosure.

"I can't stay late tonight. The kids have choir practice tomorrow for the school Christmas concert." The pastor's wife asked me to stay, and it was a difficult choice to make. However, it was already late and my little one had fallen asleep in the pew waiting for me to finish decorating the church with scenes from the nativity. I noticed Mr. Bill H. leaning against a wall, looking rather pale and sickly. "Can I get you a glass of water or something else?" I asked. I was concerned; he was always immovable. His response left me with a cold emptiness inside. "I'm not feeling well, and I have a terrible pain in my lower back." As retired military, he never complained, so this was very odd.

I didn't see him for several weeks and no mention was made during church of his wellbeing. Then the bomb dropped. From the pulpit the news was shared: Mr. Bill was diagnosed with acute lymphocytic leukemia. Silence turned into prayers, then tears as we were informed of a meal train and housekeeping needs soon to be posted.

I looked on my work phone that morning; as usual my assignments were listed. As I read down the list of names of the people I would visit today, I saw Mr. Bill's name. Hospice patient Bill H.... His condition went from bad to worse. He was placed in an acute care medical facility in Cape May. His daughter lived in California and was unable to be with him. Walking quietly into the room, I smelled the ketones, a sign of severe dehydration. I knew my job, and I knew why I was there. Generally, hospice patients receive care three hours each day for five days weekly. I kept in constant contact with his daughter and the pastor.

It was February, and my shift had ended long ago. I sensed I needed to see Mr. Bill. I knew the facility would understand my concern and allow me to visit well after visiting hours ended. I tucked my children into bed, left Gazelle in charge, and kept the phone on the entire time. We did that often.

I drove up the long drive to the parking lot; it had begun to snow. Tire tracks were left behind from the guests and staff who had just left. I brought my Bible and planned to read from the book of Proverbs, Mr. Bill's favorite. He especially like Proverbs 18:14: "The spirit of man will sustain him in sickness" (NKJV). Indeed, it did. I never knew another ill person decline as gracefully and with such poise as Mr. Bill. It was Proverbs 18:24 which Mr. Bill held so dear: "But there is a friend who sticks closer than a brother" (NKJV). I understood the meaning, but had never experienced a relationship as deep. I prayed for Mr. Bill, not for healing, but to be his friend who would be there to the very end.

The room was quiet, just past 2:00 a.m. The snow was accumulating quickly, and I was nervous for my children. Mr. Bill moaned a bit. I went to his bedside, he opened his eyes wide, sat straight up, looked at something only he saw, and collapsed back on the bed.

I called his daughter. I told her she should talk to him, say "I love you" or something, and then he was gone. It was a God moment. I felt privileged to be there for Mr. Bill as he was there for me!

• CHAPTER 13 •

The Watchman

OFTEN, I'VE THOUGHT THAT God would use me to tell people that abortion is wrong, that it is a tool Satan uses to hinder us and keep us in bondage, to increase his kingdom and simultaneously ruin the lives of women, men, and families who go through abortions. Even the clinic employees involved in abortions are impacted. At times, they too feel compromised.

I've thought that somehow God would allow me to be a voice. That is my hope and my prayer. That is why I chose to tell my children. I wanted them to hear it from me first, not to read it in a book or hear it in a conference. I owed them that much. And for me, after revealing to my children about my childhood and the abortions, I felt like I was opening the doors and clearing out the demons.

I had another experience with a sweet aroma. It occurred after I had my five children, and I was in church praying for another woman. We were laying hands on her and then the whole church suddenly smelled like roses.

We all looked around at each other wondering, *What is this? Where is this coming from?* It was odd … like somebody sprayed rose air freshener in the room. It was overwhelming, then it was gone. We knew God was there with us. And at that moment, I remembered the time on the train.

A hard heart leads us to turn away from God and to respond in disobedience and unbelief. When we do, there are consequences.

So many believe God isn't with them in the dark, in the pain and hurt. But that simply isn't true. God is with us, everywhere and always. God sees your pain. God is with you.

Those times, while I was waiting in the triage room preparing for my abortions, I felt as if I wanted to run, but I didn't. If I had responded properly at that time, if I had responded with a godly heart, I would have listened to what God was saying to me through His word. Instead, I rebelled, hardened my heart against Him, and continued with the abortions.

We do that at times in our lives. God speaks softly to our hearts, and we turn away to follow our own desires. Proverbs 14:12 tells us, "There is a way that seems right to a man, but its end is the way of death" (NKJV).

A heart that is centered on our own will is a heart that is hard. "Happy is the man who is always reverent, but he who hardens his heart will fall into calamity" (Prov. 28:14 NKJV).

> **Today, if you will hear His voice, Do not harden your hearts as in the rebellion.**
>
> —Hebrews 3:15 NKJV

A hard heart leads us to turn away from God and to respond in disobedience and unbelief. When we do, there are consequences. Even though God promises redemption, the results of our ungodly choices remain the same.

It was that way for the children of Israel (Psa. 95:6–11) and it is the same for us. The difference now is the redeeming grace we have because of the sacrifice God made in giving His Son Jesus that we may live (John 3:16). He redeems us as we turn from unbelief and turn to God. He is our hope and our Savior.

CHAPTER 14

God's Truth Revealed

SO HOW DID WE get to where we are today? How can we be so adamant about saving the trees and protecting the animals, yet continue to allow abortion and evil against humanity to exist? How can we say that personal desires are more important than a human life? We have a problem in our society, and the problem starts inside all of us. It begins in the heart when we extend the boundaries of choice to include the misguided information of a worldview that causes us to act in a detrimental way toward God's creation in the womb.

In Jeremiah 17:9 we read, "The heart is deceitful above all things, and desperately wicked: who can know it?" (KJV).

> **But the LORD said to Samuel, "Do not look at his appearance or at his physical stature, because I have refused him. For the LORD does not see as man sees; for man**

> **looks at the outward appearance, but the LORD looks at the heart."**
>
> —1 Samuel 16:7 NKJV

The heart reveals our true self to God and to others. The problem of abortion is not really a problem of society; it stems from the condition of a woman's heart. Both men and women have the power to end abortion by allowing God to change their hearts. They need to come to the realization that abortion, at its very core, is murder. It is the literal disembodiment of human life. We were all meant to live in communities, and family is a beautiful representation of community.

Abortion destroys family and community. It ends the continuation of life, and it can prevent a family from even beginning, let alone living, an abundant life. "The thief does not come except to steal, and to kill, and to destroy. I have come that they may have life, and that they may have *it* more abundantly" (John 10:10 NKJV; see also Deuteronomy 4:29; 1 Thessalonians 5:17).

Scripture also teaches us to do those things that are honorable and worth doing:

> **Finally, brethren, whatever things are true, whatever things are noble, whatever things are just, whatever things are pure, whatever things are lovely, whatever**

> **things are of good report, if there is any virtue and if there is anything praiseworthy—meditate on these things.**
>
> —Philippians 4:8 NKJV

When I talk about the word "pure," I am referring to an internal purity, a purity of the heart. Hearts turned toward God rather than toward man. The heart of man, if it does not seek the true God, seeks out idols to fill the void. When we decide to have an abortion for whatever reason, we have become the idol that we worship. An idol is anything we place in a position that usurps the supremacy of God.

> ***When we decide to have an abortion for whatever reason, we have become the idol that we worship.***

When we choose to have an abortion, we are putting our own motives first. We are putting ourselves in the position of God. Even if we are told by a doctor that the baby might be sick or have a debilitating disease and abortion is recommended so that the child would not "suffer" in life, are we really thinking about the child? Or are we thinking about the sacrifice we would have to make in raising that child?

> **And let the peace of God rule in your hearts, to which also you were called in one body: and be thankful.**
>
> —Colossians 3:15 NKJV

We are challenged by this verse to have the character of Christ in the way we relate to one another, including our relationship with the unborn child.

I recognize there are many social issues that fuel the culture of abortion: power and control, freedom of choice, medical rights, sexual freedom, quality of life, economic advancement, and liberty. All those issues flow out of a heart that is not surrendered to God. Whenever one is faced with the choice of abortion, the heart is always involved.

Just about everyone I have talked to about stopping abortion believes it is a social issue. They believe it can be prevented through legal or legislative channels and social reform. But the ultimate rule of law lies within the woman's heart. When she realizes that her womb is a safe haven, and she recognizes the life inside of her as her child, and that she is the protector of her child, that's when abortion will end. In Psalm 139:13, the writer says God was there in the beginning: "For you created my inmost being; you knit me together in my mother's womb" (NIV).

Too many people consider the woman's opinion, and perhaps the doctor's, but how many stop to consider God when it comes to abortion?

Having been involved in abortion, I know it is wrong. It is the taking of a human life. As in the psalm above, the Bible shows that life begins at conception. God fashions us in our mother's womb. God called both the prophet Jeremiah and the Apostle Paul before they were born (Jer. 1:5 and Gal. 1:15). In Luke 1:44 we are told that John the Baptist leaped in his mother's womb when the voice of Mary was heard. Obviously, from God's perspective, a child in the womb is alive.

God also condemned the Israelites who offered their children to foreign gods as sacrifices, burning them in the fire, offering them up as a sacrifice to sensuality and convenience. The same is occurring today—not by throwing our children in the fire, but through abortion—making the statement that our children are worth nothing. This is a terrible blot on our society.

Obviously, there is a difference of opinion in our society and other cultures about children and the sanctity of the womb. In some areas of the world, abortion is hardly heard of. It's considered unthinkable and cruel. Yet in China, there is abortion on demand and even forced abortion for economic reasons. There was a time when social mores made abortion highly shameful and thus a taboo subject. It is still an issue today, that is why women need healing. That is what this book is about—healing and hope. It wasn't until the seed was planted in a woman's heart suggesting that her life would be better or easier by having an abortion, or that abortion would avoid a potential problem, that the massacre of innocents began.

Throughout history and the world over, women desired to have a fruitful womb and feared being barren. How did we reach a point where a woman will now turn against herself, her natural instincts, and the purpose of her design to destroy the child inside of her? We don't even see that in the animal kingdom. A documentary on Africa recorded the case of a mother elephant that stayed behind with her drought-weakened baby, putting herself at risk of dying or being killed by predators. Another such documentary showed a mother deer fiercely attacking a mountain lion that threatened her young, repeatedly kicking the lion with her narrow hooves. Even the father penguin knows to care for the unborn, as he holds his mate's egg on his feet to keep it warm. A man may ask, "What gives a woman the right to terminate the pregnancy without discussing it with the father first?"

Abortion is not only unthinkable, but also the height of barbarity. When did we stop protecting our young?

Psalm 127:3 says, "Behold, children are a heritage from the Lord, the fruit of the womb a reward."

Everything good in my life has always come through my God. That's where it began—with my search for God. Previously, I had searched for God in all the wrong places, but I didn't know they were wrong. Now, because of Jesus in my life, I know Him, and putting Him first has allowed me to know the joy of motherhood, not once, but five times.

CHAPTER 15

How to Press On

HOW DO WE HEAL from the brokenness of a choice to abort? I can only share how I have been able to let go and heal.

1. We cannot experience full and complete healing apart from God. He is Jehovah-Rapha, the Lord Who Heals. He is the ultimate physician. Therefore, acknowledge Jesus as Savior and Lord of your life.
2. There is nothing wrong with seeking help from counselors. God has gifted Christian counselors with the words and ability to help you get beyond your disgrace and undo the emotional damage caused by your choice to abort.
3. Remember Paul's words in Philippians 3:13–14 to press on toward the call of God in your life. When he said forget, it doesn't mean you never remember the life taken. Rather, it means not to allow your ungodly choice to rule your life. No longer dwell every

day and moment on what you have done, but think on what God can do with it.

4. Pray. Ask God for forgiveness for abortion and accept that you have been forgiven. Then forgive yourself. One of the hindrances that holds us back is when we do not forgive ourselves.
5. Turn from making ungodly choices and turn to God every single day. Begin your day with that commitment to Him. "Lord, today I choose You. Lead me in Your everlasting way."
6. Ask the Lord to heal you and help you focus on the goodness of God.
7. Thank Him for allowing you to ____________. You fill in the blank.
8. Praise God for never giving up on you. Ask Him to reveal His call and purpose for your life.
9. Find a support group. Contact us at www.disgraceundone.org.

A Sample Prayer for You

Father, You knew me before I was born. Like everyone else, I came into this world and became captured by it until You set me free in Christ Jesus. But through every crisis, through every storm, through every ungodly choice

I make, I know You are with me. You have established a plan and purpose for me from the very beginning. Thank You for never giving up on me to draw me to Your redeeming grace. Amen.

Once we are ready, God lights a fire to draw us near to hear His calling on our lives. The key to the calling is to be ready to forge ahead, without the hindrance of dwelling on the past. Paul said to press on. Moses went to see how a fire could burn without burning up the bush (Ex. 3:2–5). Why did God call him at that time after forty years? Because Moses was *ready* to hear from God.

The key to the calling is to be ready to forge ahead, without the hindrance of dwelling on the past.

Are you ready to be forgiven and to forgive? Are you ready to listen when God speaks? Are you ready to press on toward the upward call of God in Christ Jesus?

CHAPTER 16

Set Free

My purpose in writing this book is not to point to me and what I have been through, but rather to point to God and to glorify Him for what He has done in my life and can do in yours. God can use our sin to bring about a greater good as we cry out to Him for restoration.

Today, I minister daily to women like us. If you are reading this book because you have suffered PASS, I encourage you to know that there is hope. His name is Jesus. He is the confident expectation of something good in your life. In Him you are forgiven. As you walk with Him, you can serve the purpose you were created for and be the woman God created you to be.

My story doesn't end here, and it didn't end when Gazelle and I were in Dunkin' Donuts.

As I washed dishes one day in 2003, I had an overwhelming urge to go to the shore and put my feet in the water. I couldn't explain what came over me, but, unexpectedly, I told the kids, "Let's go to the beach." My children were shocked because they knew I never left the dishes in the sink. They jumped up and were ready to go. They knew something special was happening.

The moment my feet touched the water, God opened the heavens, and I had a vision of a mountain with three peaks. It was overwhelming. God impressed upon my mind the verse from Habakkuk 2:3 which says, "For the vision is yet for an appointed time, but at the end it shall speak, and not lie: though it tarry, wait for it; because it will surely come, it will not tarry" (KJV).

God burned that vision into my mind, and for the next three days, I thought I was going *out* of my mind.

I began to write and draw it. I painted it on four three-by-twelve-foot canvases. Even now, I am in the process of restoring it. This was another spiritual marker for me that has led to my current ministry.

Current Ministry

The vision the Lord allowed me to see, three large mountains enveloped in the magnificent sunset of His design, left me speechless, but wondering, "What's next and why me?" Perhaps the first mountain cast a shadow of the tumultuous beginning of a life saturated in darkness. The second mountain is very steep and covered with snow. Perhaps it represents the difficulties of being a single parent, often frozen in the memories of guilt, pain, and shame, taking one step forward and slipping back three. The third peak is the future; what will I do with this opportunity?

After my last child was born, my circumstances were difficult. I had five children to provide for and I sensed regret that another marriage had ended in failure. I love being married. I love being a mom and a wife. Reading about the virtuous wife in Proverbs 31 challenged me. But that was in the past. The road I was on was lonely, desolate, and bleak. I felt hopeless. I cried myself to sleep most nights, but this night was different. God placed Isaiah 54 in my mind, and I wanted to read it. Although reading my Bible had become intentional now, I was unfamiliar with Isaiah. Although I found myself in the dark once again, this time was different. It was in the dark of night that God was showing me the light of the future He was preparing for me.

> **"Sing O barren, you who have not borne! Break forth into singing, and cry aloud, you have not labored with child! For more are the children of the desolate than the children of the married woman," says the Lord.**
>
> —Isaiah 54:1 NKJV

This led to creating the Isaiah 54 Women's Ministry, a Bible study I have facilitated and taught in churches and small groups. I also began to meet abandoned single women experiencing homelessness.

This was another spiritual marker in my life—my new life in Christ. I stepped into it with both feet and a happy heart.

Appendix A

DEPENDING ON WHICH DEVELOPMENTAL stage the trauma occurs, emotional effects can vary. This is because of brain development at a given age, which impacts the ability to reason or process the event.

A consistent thread that runs through adults who experienced childhood trauma is a tendency to compensate for the deep emotional scars in dysfunctional ways. These might include such as:

> **Passive-aggression:** The suppressing of emotions, especially of anger, is common in adults of childhood trauma. Underlying anger that remains unexpressed can result in an inability to express feelings honestly or authentically, resulting in backhanded forms of aggression or anger toward a significant other, friends, or coworkers.
>
> **Victimhood:** Having been victimized as children, in the case of childhood neglect or abuse, may result in "stuck" beliefs that once a victim, always a victim. This can lead to

adult behaviors that are based on negative self-talk and a sense of victimhood that keeps one from taking control over one's life.

Presenting a False Self: One coping mechanism for those who experience symptoms of childhood trauma in adulthood is to hide one's true self and replace it with a false self that they believe is more acceptable. Burying emotions and pretending the trauma never happened is the way they perceive themselves to have value, versus allowing the true self to emerge, which they fear may lead to rejection.

Dealing with the lasting effects of childhood trauma and abuse will require treatment to help overcome these emotional issues. Living with childhood trauma without treatment can manifest into serious mental health conditions and if left untreated can leave someone feeling hopeless and debilitated. Treatment is key for emotional trauma and childhood abuse.

Here is a common list of mental health conditions that can be treated with effective help:

Depression

Depression is common in adults with a history of childhood trauma. Unresolved emotional pain and latent fear can result in a depressive disorder. Treatment for depression involves a combination of psychotherapy as well as holistic activities that also help process pain.

Anxiety Disorder

Children who were abused or traumatized develop symptoms such as hyper-arousal of emotions, being easily startled, mood swings, and excessive fears, all hallmarks of anxiety disorder. Anxiety is treated with psychotherapy, particularly cognitive behavioral therapy, and relaxation techniques.

PTSD

Post-traumatic stress disorder results from a traumatic event that has not resolved itself. The individual becomes stuck in the memories, flashbacks, or triggers of the event which can significantly impair daily functioning and damage relationships. PTSD can be treated through various exposure therapies, eye movement desensitization and reprocessing (EMDR), and medication.

Addiction

Adults who harbor deep-seated pain from childhood are prone to using substances to help them cope with the resulting issues that arise in adulthood. Drug and alcohol addiction is treated by detoxification, rehabilitation, and various continuing care strategies that further reinforce sobriety.[2]

2 "Symptoms of Childhood Trauma in Adults," The Treatment Specialist, accessed October 24, 2022, https://thetreatmentspecialist.com/symptoms-of-childhood-trauma-in-adults/.

What's Next

I can't wait to share my next book with you about the new ministry being formed—*Disgrace Undone*. You can visit the website to be updated on hope for healing of those who are post-abortion.

www.disgraceundone.org

disgraceundone4u@gmail.com

What's Next

I [illegible] WANTED TO share my next book with you about the new [illegible] —? [illegible] [illegible] the website to be updated [illegible] hope [illegible] those who are most [illegible]

[illegible]

[illegible]